MY THOUGHTS

Naveed Akram

Order this book online at www.trafford.com
or email orders@trafford.com

Most Trafford titles are also available at major online book retailers.

Printed in the United States of America.

ISBN: 978-1-4669-4066-6 (sc)
ISBN: 978-1-4669-4067-3 (hc)
ISBN: 978-1-4669-4065-9 (e)

Library of Congress Control Number: 2012909816

Trafford rev. 05/30/2012

 www.trafford.com

North America & international
toll-free: 1 888 232 4444 (USA & Canada)
phone: 250 383 6864 ◆ fax: 812 355 4082

Poetry for the soul. Designed to inspire the mind.

CONTENTS

PRATTLE

I paddled for a while in the living
Quarters, that are so righteous.
The rooms dwindled away, and I
Spoke some sound for the epics.
The interview was brief, and expert,
Like the houses to be built.
My opening fight opposed me
As conversations rushed on
With the words blundering and bouncing.

A little prattle worsened the mood,
Moods were attitudes of great zeal.
The master of the school was a hapless
Individual, concentrated in confusion and crying.
My prattlers at home would complain,
After the days of your vomit
And pies of heaven inside the mind.

I pounced on workers of ancient history,
The Latin and Greek turned into water
As the classical trees became uprooted,
Like a magnificent tune or fit of music,
As many notes as you want.

My Mind

This well in my mind swallows water,
I confess to sins of liquidity and fluidity;
Munching the sense of knowledge
Was mastering the way you drank it,
The wisdom just poured on, letting me
Be my master of words and thoughts.

This bucket is full of words, converted
And fully apt for the job of language.
You must take your fill, washing the teeth
So well, that wellington boots are worn
On the toes bespeaking.

The water has arrived erroneously, I swear.
Knowing me is like conducting a service
To polite individuals of similar rank.

The living mind cannot contain the real bite
So lent to the banks of opportunity.
The paper of this press confides in me,
As does feline company, the clever ones
Who intimidate the young and fill
Geniuses with hatred.

This well in my head shatters the heart from
The heat, accusing me of sacred blessings
And banks of talking thoughts called philosophy.

My mind is made to fun, my brain speaks to it,
As far as my imagination is certain and definite.
The speaking is like condemnation from court,
Fiddled with the words of non-meaning.

The heavy trance of slices
Carries on the time of the brain,
Gray matter and white matter
Are confused in the elixir of intelligence.

WORTH

I intended a poem of worthiness,
And it turned out to be prosaic in nature.
When first the words lengthened
We excited the judiciary,
Like the masters have done.

These many freedoms watch,
As a crack of the page is begun,
To feel mighty words is an honour
For the swift-at-heart.

Paddies begin and matter to the rich
Who clothe themselves in rice and water;
Poor ones resent this act of their distinction.
My field is alone and without words,
Dancers gaze tonight for more revels.

I intend to write my fortune in this fist
Looking away as I watch the preview
Of the film in question, to be this right
Is like an offering of the sacred kind.

Mighty words happen tonight,
Today my fighters stage a rebellion,
Fixing my eyes on their minds.

My Weapon

To see my weapon you must fight with it,
To gaze at the victory we watch politely,
Yet my goals with the gods are twofold,
And far too gladdening like the sport of the soul.

My soul reaches into the world,
Gazing helplessly at the void,
Enjoyed, by a humanoid.

Let the souls of hysteria will their magic,
Metals concern me with the Periodic Table.
So the chemist spies on the humans
With his joy, and weapon.
The Table spells the nymph
Like the naked prince, and the full heat
Of the fire is eight times the sun.

Cardiac surgery makes me overjoyed,
Love has entered the readiness of our life,
The doctors are niggardly displacing the brain,
Forming work for their brains,
Let cranes be lanes for the overwhelmed few.
This theatre is of the peace that
The heart has passed.
It poses a penitence so of slaves,
Grains spill to hide the guilt,
In fashion of the times that maintain.

Hurricanes support me,
Weapons launched bitterly detest me.

A GREAT GATE

Attain the blessings of a great gate,
The planes have ceilings of a great gate.

Forming the periods of the times
Is like finding the clearings of a great gate.

To see nails into the splintered blocks of wood
Is of the time we have the coverings of a great gate.

This colour mutters of course in mild uniform,
Then clocks override the system of belongings, of a great gate.

The real subtlety is in factories of tools,
Charts of stunts on walls and killings, of a great gate.

This life must have wings of homeliness,
Life functions again when with lashings of a great gate.

My names are the drink of my soul,
Life shall be colourful once the hatred has leanings of a great gate.

CLEAR MISERY

I am a marvel to my grand-children,
In the dour ages that lie there irate.
My marvels sell the diaphanous chapters
Of my dear, dear life.
Is this the one catching my wish?
My wishes function internally,
Do not be mean to my misery.
Let the one so adored be my misery.
I know why gaping holes excite
The communist historians.
I do not know snipers in the mist,
They cause me to exert modernity.
The historical meaning is encapsulated,
By my gods of liberty.
The abbot shall return and sweet showers
Of hell shall rain to keep my spell.
This meaning carries out the window,
My window speaks tonight.
Let this, I am sure the nights are too long
Like loaves of bread.
Misery has entered.

STORMS OF HATE

Do not be mean to storms of hate,
I killed myself gladly of veils and smells
Loitering and staining me with odours soporific.
I sleep due to man, who weighs heavily
On my mind, inside the dreamscape tonight.
But it shimmers inside the bed,
The world will go up in a shriek,
I am terrified, for to give it up is sleep.
If you only know the wide and deep feelings,
Welcoming my glad offering.
Offered are the odorous sniffs,
Slipping below a bed of heaven.
Let this be death in its finality,
The real religious notion of our age.

Ages shall keep heavenly messages;
I do not want much of a present,
Do not be irritating to my folly and vice,
That glimmer and gladden me now and then.

OF DANGER

To evacuate the soul I turn to follow a spy,
Working methodically and plentifully.
A black tumble of rocks makes me mad,
With a crunch, on the crown of the cloud.
I tore a mouthful of weed, crouching carefully
To intimidate the other person, my lovely neighbour.
There were strange pictures painted on my lap,
The plaster wall was absent,
The wall of steel was present.
The left hand at her arm was pleasant,
With a blunt stone the fire started
With a status of danger.

Curious, the steel of the hand transformed
Into spines of luck, a reality had deformed,
The real bunch of banners were bought by the eye,
I am sure it was unique.

Satanic Star

This coastland is mean to my unique body,
Do not mean this surprising and surpassing detail.

Take my bed and sleep, take it in your hand,
And then sit, with this coastland of details.

The soil is bland, far against the devil,
But no threatening details became president.

The soil warmly smiles at the distinct sun,
In this computer land there is a brand new star.

It causes a surrender, the feelings of awe
Surprise me, as cans of water feed me.

She blinked, cleaning the blade,
Watching a book from a distance.

This is a question of pain, a pleasant suffering
Of sweat and supermen, the opposite of danger.

This coastland remade me after twice the heat,
This star satanically remarks on the soul.

BUSINESS
WITH VIRTUE

Why do hills become business matters?
This is a question of strength and virtue,
May the answers run fully with abolishers.

This sentence reminds me of addressers,
A real mind connected each avenue,
Why do hills become business matters?

The leaders of the sand damage a union of forgivers,
This damnation starts so as to argue,
May the answers run fully with abolishers.

It proceeds forward, the animal is awake with fortune-tellers,
I have argued with trust and said my clue,
Why do hills become business matters?

A canoe waits tonight, to see me cry with fractures,
Well hidden are the lies of disastrous jujitsu,
May the answers run fully with abolishers.

This night passed forming unions and founders,
The truth has occurred like an issue,
Why do hills become business matters?
May the answers run fully with abolishers.

STARTLED MAN

Startled, he pricked his thumb,
What noise beckoned his pleasure?
Casting spells of disaster became outside,
Staining it, saving it, and being windows.

Behind him, he heard bad trouble,
Picking himself up, he heard and saw the trouble.
Do not be mean to him, realise why it was him?
Bringing lanterns to the door
Was his pleasure.

Wait. His paint blew across the mirror,
Light appeared at the archways;
Glazed with the lust of blood,
Walls seemed showing of themselves.

He cried. Causing hectic sound,
Sibilant torture, fulfilments and enjoyment
From others, who had pricked the
Wrong shoe.

He cried eternally in his sleep,
Did he want to be killed?
No. His progeny would have loved
Him.

COMPOSER

Who was the composer of joy?
Differing theories analysed this.
Why the closer? Why another dimension?
The reality of elusive sergeants
Seemed like the appearances
To be announced by the devilry.
I could describe the harmonic progressions,
The heart of the mystery laid open.
After the chamber-music a laugh
Emerged for the submarines of cancer.
The gathering dust understood how late
The situation became in the light of danger.

The keeper swore as my mother shone,
The father wept as a key fell into the lock
With clicks, more clicks and justice an duty.

He sat under the name of a physician,
My mother shone, like suns and stars
Due to health, the emergency stayed.
Agitated, a concealment showed a light
And darkness coming from the tapping of tyres.

SPLASHING
THE WATER

Starlight glinted off the water,
Hyder sat up abruptly with a film of sweat;
Startled, he accessed films and movies
Of life.
With this pond of sweat around his arteries,
He measured the vibrations,
Waiting and thrashing, twisting and splashing,
His powerful tail beamed on the beef
And lava of the cadaverous livid body
That he possessed.
An introduction was needed in a second.
A strength was determined by history
And its providers.

Running shoes splashed on the water,
This water was in the open air.
Gazing at the hand of God,
He worked hard to splash and ignite
Fervour and strength
In the zealots of the East.

DEEPER SHARKS

Massive sharks jump to the ground,
Screaming fortunate cries it sounds like
A torturer in the water, with
Tortuous tracks and lethal traps
Of longer wars and shoulders and fins.
The rush of air furiously finds fault
With fanatics of the fun water.
Exposing me, the sharks of the great sea
Should demand money and honey.
As the teeth closed a thrust was heard,
Blood had emerged for the emergency,
The real accident of the holiday season.

This news made me cry,
Lamentation swiftly adored me
As misery took the fish of the great sea
By the fin and slashed its head with blunt
Instruments.

Spray washed over a man who fond it,
The blood was black and took the waves
With seasons of laughter,
Panels beneath the belly.

May jumping sound far too great,
In the thrust of the deep-blue sea.

LEAVING US

Raise my scratch to elevate the ranks,
A tonnage of kisses alleviates the suffering,
Suggesting the furies of levitation,
Inside this goal of your happiness.

Demonic winds connect us to the despair
And so sense appears to read us
In the papers of a sage who is rich,
Infecting real knowledge.

The infrequent waves desist,
Denigrating the ways,
Keeping dire delays of strength,
Dangerously leaving us.

Repel the traitor now and then,
To appease the enemy
For their laughter is immense.

WICKED RAID

A wicked raid commences now for you,
This battle made me work like something cool,
A wicked raid commands the avenue
That you still proffer from, that molecule.

A little way casts soldiers acting so,
The only stay we make can craft the acts,
These actions spell like words too much ago,
Inside me I have seen some artefacts.

The real men came, the real men satisfied
Us when they said that we were bold as balls,
A ready wail contained me and complied
Instead the regions won, like bitter falls.

I wed the bride of liberty, of strain,
This strain and freedom made my little brain.

Door To Youth

How open is the door to youth?
My truth carries on further for you,
For you are as young as candlelight,
Yesterday was a sin, a day to be forgotten.
Please forgive the occasion,
And please me further with truth,
This truth hurts me while the heart murmurs,
Moaning as a dense nerve.

Don't dawdle and deliver praise,
Like this be heavenly, and receive a joy
To be wide and deep like meanness,
Do not be certain of my brainy statements,
This law hides me as a law,
This law is of laws.

Loud is the laughter, and laudable is the cosiness
We are in, the cute babies celebrate:

My Acts

My sentences betray the philosophy inside my country of weakness,
The strong results beam on a system itself, that reads forever and forever.
This day we make a fortune from forms and fulfilling frowns of fright,
I have this day as a day of light, the light of the dark is extreme.
Call the men with supermen on their minds, the bosses stay this way,
Making major fidgets, boiling the minds with mental thoughts
That are like strings and knots, but without knots.
This thought delivers my acts and they have united the world
When witches stare into space and time, to deliver their elixir.

I may see meals of different colours, of different sizes and slices,
But you differ on the lives you lead, lessening the load and love.
My meals like flowers betray the sun, with their full covers
And hungry-looking traits, a trait may be eaten like a real religion.

Shocking Missiles

A vituperative statement composes my fury,
Fury shall make me wear a frown.
A virtue vanishes, a real religion emerges
With the light of the train and the teacher.
This knowledge masters my matter like mathematics
Solved again and again, repetitions are a help.
This water is a vapour in the middle of a law,
Letters follow with the pen that writes.

Let it be a forcibility that describes success,
Into the deep pits we go, like shocking missiles.
The missiles connect to believe, and this is belief,
For we cause a ready region.

The diseased mildew infects my head and heart,
This stated the obvious to be me,
This said to me a picture of great glory.

REMIND US

An useful tenet describes my knowing command,
Leaders of fortune delay their expressions of hate.

They lie when the liars drool, they speak by way of mouth
To innocent eye, a pair of ears enjoys the man who leads.

Lists of pains and pleasures cannot be life to be meaningful,
Do not request a detail to be delayed far off.

My cards are numbered in the dozens,
These cause me to ask a maker to canter and toss.

The real cards ease the expressions of heat,
Really the reasons of error are numberless.

Let this be a lesson for wicked puppies
In the meaningful phrases of a box.

The boxes of animals are parcelled to all,
For the right of a citizen reminds us.

Let the criminals of this age be a gain and brain
Forming us as we stare in the real religion.

HEARING

To harry me is to belabour the whole body,
Opening foreign affairs to the public;
The country's truth leads me to sins
That love me, as I love the synod of beliefs.

My acts are a variety to the bleeding brothers,
Needing a prosperity of years that are overfeeding;
Careers consider the effects of whole diseases,
Then the worries desist, they overwork,
As this day is alive with the sounds of heaven.

To halves the seeds are split, a pursuit splits,
Like the heavenly bridges leading to Hell.

I love the stages of the aspects given to houses,
Their smiles enjoy me as a entrance
Into the jaws of a passageway,
Welling up, so swollen is the mud of the hut.

I have acted righteously, and you must really feed
On those who domineer on those endearing others,
The gears interfere, like a mad rush,
Of ears hearing the hearers.

BOMBARDIERS

Bombardiers spoil the career of electioneers,
Hell feels like an eggshell to be explosive,
With decibels and farewells of the expulsion.
Cromwell feels safe today, now that he dwells
With the ground and sees a futuristic image
Ready to expand.

To this band of heroes my flatland is in dispute,
A fairyland shall appear with a grandstand
Gruelling in its patient activity of standing and sitting
For the really displaced citizens.

They are found in dykes and horrid conditions,
Settlements are hats for the bands of warriors;
These occasions split the fires,
With any sort of hazards.

Ashtray

This ashtray closes in on the victim,
An archway affords a man with a woman,
The cabaret contains a buffet with a carriageway,
The bray of the music makes me dizzy
Like a restaurant in spoiling luxuries.

The chalice extraordinarily menaces that chalice of silver,
Aides adorn the additions called subtractions,
Harmonizing is the key.

The headquarters head us, thinking by the secrets
Shaking along a fussy river of wholesome bread
Earned by the benefactors of the nation.

Then hate the luxury entertaining me today,
Healing my prison, heaving and shivering;
Like headwaiters.

The stepdaughter of life shall congratulate the teas
Experienced by them, the seawater absorbs us;
May we be underwater forever.

Plots are afoot, like otters, in the sea of tranquillity
Those folks have in their hands.

PRISON IS A PRIZE

I found the muscle-bound soldier as a warrior,
Dumb as the bricks on water and mud,
Bound for the prison that is a prize,
I am drowning.

This reality was eastern, and in the tin of the west
We bang and change the tatters of our fanged metals;
The accidents of this folly are numberless,
Encumbering the ice of this cloud,
Greyhounds enter the clearing,
Hounds find their shouts of liars.

After all, they have dined and sat in a swept cloud
Forming a new reason for living,
Mines are afoot to be intertwined
And underlining the feet of our victims.

The masterminds open their pages to consult
The moons for their own conversation
To be guilty and depraved like a departed soul.

Inspired By Forests

Inspirer of the woods commended me for acts of bravery;
Able, acoustical and lovely, he demanded no more forests.
I was accountable for my deeds that ran in the thousands,
"Off to the cells!" he said as an act of slaying.

In the prison-cell of pyramids my actions spoke,
Assisting others with like-minded problems.
Their talents were dependable on habits,
And O God did they detach their tone from me.

After the refresher's course, my talent grew
To side with evil, the loosened of all the wits;
Deploring dangerously, he went over the ground
To arrest me in my land of endeavours.

Where stood the stowaways of life?
The devoted among them stayed longer,
Only one way was there decision-making,
In this respect their auction was over.

CHEMICALS

The chemicals in my mouth exploded with triumphant
Scents and odours, that weapons of distrust developed
Into the arms and legs, fully charged with infantry.

The demonstrations hid depression once denial kept,
Dividing sacred blocks of stone cancelled my answers,
By the way, a block of wood weighed far too little.

To be delighted is a scary proposition, and enemies
Run into the city to massacre a nation's pride;
The denominations stung the houses of proud men;
Women and children, politicians and lawyers,
Had attained old youth, a victim of contemplation.

The scares grew like bacteria in their place of reasons,
The deposed leader sank to the floor of cabarets,
Much lingual expertise had delivered praise.

MY POLICY

I have a department
Foreign to you as me,
Dental implants waste me.
To be teeth confuses me,
Divide this scary book,
Devote yourself to us.
My deputies should live
Longer than red ruin,
Detecting the slightest.
My policy demands
That you deliver this
To my boss who scans me.
The needle of distaste
Pictures body after corpse
In this unique setting.
The demons resent our
Food that travels against
The stream of new hope here.
Must we devise a toy
To better another?
No, not now that we shine.

Then Rejoice

The abdomen mimics an accordion
Paying for my music with food that collects.
The crayon of coolness climbs like a Cuban cigar
Into the mouth of folly.

My cousin is tamed by the cigars of joy,
My familiar habit is contagious considerably.
Let craftsmen utter creation with their tongues
And not just their throats.

The dandelions are lit by foxes
In a trail of outspoken cleverness.
Their real craft loathes just crustaceans
As crewmen astound you more like this.

Then crimes cannot be mistaken,
Theft of an object must be spoken about
To achieve the highest forms of awesome pleasure,
To attain the position of a grand palace.

MY NUMBERS
ARE WANDS

My wands are numerous for numbers,
As their goals are tiny like the fodder of wolves;
As simply as the sea has moved, we do move,
In ways of human disorder and devastating shapes.

I live among the stones bombarding the beers,
The cans just smell from the rivers of mud,
Marshes resonate with offerings of sludge,
A shipwreck is about, it is about us.

My wandering few inhabit the devils of design,
Their lairs end up in the meanings of nonsense,
The senses of the mind entails another sense
Of logic, of logical mathematics.

Solutions
To Problems

He will maraud my being with thrown objects,
Inside their voice are joint clauses,
Internal anger fuels the conclusions,
These conclusions are my fault.

Let answers evolve with the universe,
The solutions to problems remain unknown
As long as the virtues of designing an act
Seem huge.

There is a magic of offence, the magical way
To alleviate the drudgery and sluggish Morse,
We must decode it, we must decode it,
Like the decipherers at war with the enemy.

My lands are naming a few soldiers,
Wars carry on like the dust of disease,
These wars hardly live with us
After a new hardship arrives.